Also by A.M. Hayden

American Saunter: Poems of the U.S.

How to Tie Tobacco

Advance Praise for *Old World Wings*

In *Old World Wings*, Hayden takes readers on a sensory journey through Italy, France, Eastern Europe, and Ireland. This collection blends poetry with travelogue, fine art history, religion, and popular culture. While Hayden guides us through some of Europe's most popular attractions, such as Père Lachaise Cemetery and Notre Dame Cathedral, she also goes beyond the well-known tourist sites. We observe street performers in Italy, visit a skate park in Vienna, enjoy warm sunrises and relish musical history in Austria, but the landscape darkens as we travel further east, with "Eastern Europe" perhaps the most poignant of the collection, bearing witness to one of the darkest periods in Europe's history. In the "Ireland" section, history becomes personal as Hayden considers her own place in the Irish diaspora. Old World Wings offers an outstanding view of Europe that avoids the romanticized and cliched depictions of the continent seen in so many romance novels and popular films.

~**Natalie Welsh**, Founding Editor, Syncopation Literary Journal

A.M. Hayden transports the reader with lush landscape, evolving in surprising line breaks and enjambment, transforming nouns into verbs: "firelight / your woods,", and "magic mushroom / us", and "pollen dust / these violet wildflowers." One of the compelling conflicts raised is the intention of humans toward the world. The surprise she creates compels a reader to delve more deeply into the relationship between humans and the spiritual and natural worlds, especially as embodied in cultural folk lessons. In doing so, Hayden seems to create a desire for peaceful co-existence with spiritual and natural mysteries in a destructive human world. The reader is caught up Hayden's musical language and imagery, a spell almost unto itself: "…dance / over the drumlins and burlap briar hum / your wingspans like starlings, shapeshift / against clear light o sky, hobnob, bewitch / us, spin dew into shimmer…" There is much to admire here. I thank the poet for transporting me.

~ **Dawn Terpstra,** Poetry Editor, River Heron Review

The tradition of poetry in Irish culture is as enduring and dependable as the Atlantic waves that wash the island, and the rain that keeps it misty and boggy and ethereal. A.M. Hayden's evocative and atmospheric poems veer between the ancient and the contemporary but never lose their reverence of landscape and of mood, their rigorous language of sensuality and powerful sensation. She has understood, as all who write about Ireland must do, that, as Heaney wrote, 'the wet centre is bottomless'. It is other worlds and linguistic calisthenics, it is light and shade and ageless, timeless sensation that is gossamer and fleeting, therefore challenging to corral into tidy verse. There is no substitute for visiting Ireland, but a journey with Hayden through these poems comes close, and I salute her for turning such adventures into such robust and muscular verses. *Comhghairdeas!*

~ **Dr. Niamh Hamill,** Director, Institute of Study Abroad Ireland, Co-Author of *Finding Ireland*

OLD WORLD WINGS

Poems of Europe

A.M. Hayden

A Wild Ink Publishing Original
wild-ink-publishing.com

Copyright © 2025 A.M. Hayden
Design by Abigail Wild
Layout by A.M. Hayden
Cover Photo and all other photography by A.M. Hayden

Credits

Grazie, Merci mille fois, Děkuji, and *Go raibh maith agat* to the editors who first chose to publish/select the following poems, often in earlier versions.

- Tangled Locks Journal, *"*Women have always said they are Sorry (Marie I)"[1]; "Fertilizer"

- Instant Noodles, "How to Find Jim Morrison's Grave"

- Authortunities, "Lovely Luminosity of the Italian Language"

- Rowayat International Journal, "Umbrellas and Crosses"

- Fevers of the Mind, Truth Lies, Blasphemy, and Disorder, "Memento Mori II (Depeche Mode)"

- Shine Poetry, "When You said "No" to Seeing the David[2]"; "Old Men Don't Cry (Song of Arranmore)"

- Flora Fiction, "When I Learned Enya's Castle was 20 minutes away"; "Wild Nights on the Seine"; "Café de Flore"; "Czech Student's Art Apartment"

- Sunflowers Rising Anthology (for Ukraine), Lies About How Your 17-Year-Old Brother Died (the Troubles),

- Loud Coffee Press, "Hemingway"

- Edith Chase Poetry Anthology, "Cavan Burran"

- Cool Beans Lit, "Sligo Bookstore"

- Cold River Press, Voices Anthology, "How to have a Mystical Experience"; "Café de Flore"; "I See You (St. Teresa in Ecstasy)"

---

[1]National Poetry Month Featured Poem
[2]Nominated for Pushcart Prize

- Flights Literary Magazine, "School of Athens"; "Robin Williams in a Venice Taxicab"

- Uncensored Ink, "School of Athens"

- The Apologist, "Plans"[3]

- Wayfarer Magazine, "Franceska"

- When the River Speaks, "Welsh Solstice"; "Wishing Chair"; "Waterfall Song"

- Ohio Bards Anthology, "Czech Castles, Krakow Churches"

- New Beats Generation, Nat'l & Int'l Goddess Anthology, "Hugging Nun at the Sacré Coeur"

- Ohio Writers Association, Should this Book be Banned? "Sex Museum Villanelle (*Musee d'erotique*)"

- Syncopation Literary Journal, "Epic Immigration Abecedarian"; "Latin Quarter"; "How to Find Jim Morrison's Grave"; "Now I See (Notre Dame before the Fire)"; "Smells like the Sistine Chapel"; "A Nietzschean Response to St. Patrick"[4]

- River Heron Review, "Roma Museum"[5]; "The Faery Bridges"[6]

- Lothlorien Poetry Journal, "Shamrock Wool"; "Druid Salmon" "Ogham"; "Heaven in a Long Room"; "Book of Kells"

- Milk and Cake, Dead of Winter Anthology, "Krampus and Cider"

- Lefty Blondie Press, "Bonfire of the Vanities (Venus)"[7]

---

[3] National Poetry Month Featured Poem
[4] Syncopation Literary Journal's Special Feature
[5] River Heron Review *Poetry Prize* Finalist
[6] River Heron Review *Editors' Choice Prize* Winner
[7] Lefty Blondie Press *Editors' Choice Broadside Series* Semi-Finalist

Table of Contents

FRANCE (Paris and Versailles)

EASTERN EUROPE (Austria, Czech Republic, Poland)

IRELAND (Donegal and Ireland's Northwest Region)

For Jimmy,

without you, none of it

I Do Not Know

where the sea will be,
so, we'll just keep on moving
until there's no land

ITALY

(Rome, Firenze, Venice)

2   Old World Wings

Lovely Luminosity of the Italian Language

There is only one answer in Italy
when asked, how are you? *Molto bene*
very well, thanks for asking, how could I not be?
turn around, my warmed back to the Trevi,
fling a good toss of a euro coin behind me
gilded renaissance wish of *Campo di Fiori*
the Colosseum, the Pantheon, and Vatican City
take me down where the Sistine Chapel is so pretty
with exquisite, adorned walls smelling of rosemary
and old smoke like the guy leaning over his balcony
displaying his cigar and Italian flag proudly
I could not have prepared for *St. Teresa in Ecstasy*
breathtaking pierced love in Bernini's divine beauty
she seeks my heart all day until I see David Bowie
whisper *yes, siesta*, sexy time at the chic ristorante
where spinach swims in a luxurious olive oil sea
Italian's winged words are honey buzz flutter bees
Per favore, arrivederci, grazie, sto bene
no other language could ever sound so lovely

Bernini's Fountain

Of the four rivers
your favorite is the Nile
because he shyly hides
his head, inviting the Piazza's
pleasantly perching pigeons

6   Old World Wings

Bonfire of the Vanities (Venus)

All burned
    the frivolous
        the nonreligious
            windy Wednesday
                ashes turned
                    sea phoenix
                    gusting on
              frothy waves
            swaying dreaming
        yolk painted
sunset eggs
creamy thick
        fem fertility
            lemon castration
                shelled Botticelli

"And the Flames Rose Up"

right here, where this stone pedestal
now ascends, engraved plinth
in place of the stake
strapped to Brno's body, Astronomer
condemned for his deduction
of life's possibilities on other planets
for writing poems of stars as distant suns
treacherous thoughts igniting Inquisition's
wrath, charred alive as kindling
for his sum of knowledge
Philosopher's perils of questioning
is it coincidence this was time's
same tunnel Caravaggio
captured light and dark?

10   Old World Wings

Fig Leaf Campaign

Il Braghettore
"breeches painters"
fig leaves
drape cloths
hide hanging
flesh bits
haphazard coverups
ruthless campaign
carries to
Pope's Apartment
Constantine's Vision
fiery cross
Milvian's Bridge

How to Have a Mystical Experience in Venice

                              Order seafood, scallops
specifically, a whole *plate* of scallops
watch with eager eyes as the waitress sets down
two tiny pearl pillows, each delicately placed
in the open half of its hard Botticelli
Venus shield resting on a beautiful earth green
bed of exquisite oil-dripping spinach leaves
spear the right marine bivalve mollusk
into your mouth, moan
moan again, deeper, in realization you will never
be able to enjoy seafood again after this
                              how to describe
                    a stabbing by the sublime?
seeing through time and space
saints have tried through the centuries
St. Aquinas, after years of toil, concluded all his writing
feeble straw, yet you would grab Aquinas by his collar
and show him proof here in this celestial butter bathed
sacred sharkskin manna placed gently into fleshy
soft palms of a perfectly curved Renaissance curtain
                              divine communion
                    melted on your tongue
eyes rolling up like Bernini's St. Teresa in Ecstasy,
like Uma Thurman licking
her five-dollar *Pulp Fiction* milkshake,
grateful in this moment you do not yet know
that scallops clap their shells
together like sturdy toddler hands,
use jet propulsion, have rings of eyes,
developed nervous system, do not yet know
when another saint, Augustine, watched a boy
pouring water at the seashore

                         using a similar husk,
                    attempting to empty
the sea, he knew we could never capture
or contain the enormity, the uncanny mystery
of the holy trinity, though we maniacally
clap our insignificant hands
anyway, take comfort that if not you
who consumed
on this shadowy Venetian evening
then a hungry red starfish for certain
and while starfish may be just as capable, or more,
of a celestial, mystical experience aflame
                              you savor tonight,
                    it is you

Gondola

1

Canal homes in twist
Marco Polo, Vivaldi
belly of the fish

2

Liquid corridors
red ribboned sunhats, striped shirts
rhythmic creak of oars

3

Slippery slime hull
doors, windows open and close
sweating from sun's heat

18   Old World Wings

I See You (St. Teresa in Ecstasy)

I see you, eyes rolled
          up, parted mouth
             stabbed
        by gold leaf
     spear aflame plunged into
your steampunk saint's
         heart, how do heaven
             and earth
        float midair?
    Sola fide
I see you, swooning
         back lit by ecstasy
            arrow
      drawn out
   utterly consumed
sweet pleasure
        exquisite pain
          Sola gratia
      baroque theater
   Santa Maria Del Vittorio
I see you, penetrate
      her heart
        Sola scriptura
     in ritual repetition

Sola fide (faith alone); *Sola gratia* (grace alone); *Sola scriptura* (scripture alone)

On *Vaporetti,* the Couple behind me

are speaking
not Italian,
maybe Hebrew…Arabic? distinct from all the long
vowels I have lived on and lived for.
"We just arrived!" they exclaim excitedly when we discover
      we are heading to the same hotel.
"We are from Israel!" they offer.
I'm from Ohio, I say,
the man laughs, "I was *just* in Ohio two weeks ago for work.
Dayton. Do you know Dayton?"
I nod, at him, at these butterfly wings,
      at these rippling
webbed connective strings
fused across oceans
until they both wave as they head to their room,
he turns, happily shouts:
              "I love the Air Force Museum!"

Painted Black Pieta

Rolling Stones
cover band
wild singer
sloshed crowd
dripping sweat
setting sun
swigs Schweppes
summer clothes
Michelangelo's hands
painted flowers
sculpted Mary
twenty-seven
years old
red door
bad ass
first gig

Lingerie Tanka

lingered breath whisper
lacy bits of lingerie
Firenze silk slips
soft as the pigeons' feathers
tucked underneath tender plumes

Old World Wings

The Pity (Pieta)

No halos, no crosses
in her massive frame, she cradles her limp son
a waxing moon, reaching her hand to us

No halos, no crosses
no plunging arrows, no over the top angels
all a mother's mourning of her boy lying mute

No halos, no crosses in her massive frame,
she cradles her limp son, a waxing moon

Not quite as luminous behind bulletproof glass
What a pity Our Lady is caged as she mourns

Not quite as luminous behind bulletproof glass
the geologist ran down the aisle waving a hammer
whacked Mary's nose, declared himself Messiah

Not quite as luminous behind bulletproof glass
What a pity Our Lady is caged as she mourns

Toe-Ku Kiss

Cherub angels hug holy water of Mass, where Peter
was crucified upside down, world's largest martyr's church
in smallest country built by coliseum stones, arched ceiling
would tower Statue of Liberty, Renaissance adorned with gilded
scripture six feet raised, Bernini canopy and curves echoing
with mosaics, marble, and monuments to men, men,
so many men

under golden dome
tallest in Rome, rubbed to smooth
nub, St. Peter's toe

If Khalil Gibran Visited the Duomo

before the train existed to cross
they laid railways across the alps
leap of faith in every sprawling tongue track

before the dome, they left a wide-open mouth
fourteen years later in blonde Firenze
Michelangelo lifted his face to shining Duomo

confessed St. Peter's would never be as stunning
what a miracle to build the tracks, leave the breach,
trust in time and live the questions of fortune's fate

Smells like the Sistine Chapel

No photography allowed, tourist paparazzi flashes sear eyes of choking crowd, humans are *loud*, my eyes swim and my breath heaves, lungs spilling over cherubs' cup, official business, Pope commissioned, Michelangelo insisted, *I'm not a painter,* sculpture creations that burned his heart must be put on hold for later, because you can't just say no to the Pope, so he fever washed 5,000 square feet in fresco, my Pez dispenser neck starts to ache, fig leaves and drape cloths church added to prevent perverts from thinking unsavory thoughts, and this had to twist bitter Michelangelo into knots, shoulders stretched across his make shift scaffold, holding brushes like lifting boulders for four long years, back jacked forever so you and I and every tourist can hear the music of the spheres, can follow Genesis' gestation story down to *The Last Judgment*, fresh hellish and gory, background bright cobalt blue, altar wall under Pope's smoke signals, displaying a theatric slew of frightening scenes painted years after Protest and Reform, distinct from ceiling, swarmed by unfortunate souls taken to hell, dark and tortured, deviating from his heaven where angels dwell, Michaelangelo was older then, painted his own face into the martyr's flayed skin

like the artist-formerly-known-as-Prince scrawling "slave" across his dissident cheek, because you can't stop burning brilliance, look up, right here, bright and clear, God and Adam, reaching for each other, mostly God doing the reaching to Adam, who looks like he can't find his car keys or figure out where he sat them or like he was nodding off until God interrupts, poking his Divine finger, *Humankind, wake up!* God the one making all the effort and I think of my Dad who drove me to get my passport and asked me if I was going to see the "pull my finger one," *of course*, I said, he was my Tuscan sun, I make my way toward chapel's steeple, slow shuffle through stifling stuffed blankets of people, I kneel bare summer shins to the cool marble floor, inhale Michealangelo's trippy visual memoir, I want to sprawl out, make marble angels under his stars, just for a minute, lay on my back like he did, imagine his scars, but all around me, voices echo, cameras flash, shoes squeak and I am reminded *he was 33* when he started this ceiling and *I* am 33 *right now* sitting here, which leaves me with a quite inadequate feeling, but my palms rest on my thighs, my legs tingle and fall asleep, my eyes still scan every scene, certain if frescoes made music, they would play cellos and violins, and if scratch and sniff, they'd smell of naked flesh, velvet robes, and Jasmine.

36   Old World Wings

Belieber Bell

to climb 414
steps to Giotto
Tower's top to see
Firenze's rugged
celestial 14th century
brass bell, beautiful
and majestic, only to
find *Justin Beiber* scratched
into its lipped curve
you can't belieb it

Robin Williams in a Venice Taxicab

When I ask this cab driver how he likes living here, he shrugs,
"Eh, it's just the same, 41 years, so boring, nothing's changed"
who would not want to live in a sinking stinking city
of 12 million tourists, high-rise apartments spoon bent

over liquid streets, centuries stench surface dredged
by summer's heat, "the whole place smells like a giant fart,"
he sniffs, "but I love Vietnam movies, the ones from the 80's.
Have you seen *Full Metal Jacket*?" Um, hell yes.

"*Apocalypse Now*?" Of course. I volley back, *"Platoon?"*
to his *whoop* in gruff timbre, "Oh, but the best one -
Good Morning Vietnam! I LOVE Robin Williams!
Do you like Robin Williams?" and wish I would

have been quick enough to say, *you'd be Venetian
blind to not like Robin Williams,* but it is enough
to swing sweet admiration back and forth
while watching sparkles of St. Mark's square

                         come closer, closer still

40   Old World Wings

Skeleton Stilettos in St. Mark's Square

11th century marble picture frames of Genesis
mirrored mosaics, ruby altars, pearls, and amethysts

jewels are not what made this a pilgrimage place
St. Mark's smuggled bones whisper in this space

12 centuries, pickpocket central, the karmic irony
smooth thieves, swift fingers in rose dim sanctuary

nooks and crannies of this creaky, damp refuge
a place to easily hide the weapon, deep in deluge

or the body from Doge's Palace in "elegant decay"
to the Scalzi, where the barefoot stay

the immigrants selling illegal bags to tourists
women stiletto stumbling over cobblestone to trysts

slips of fabric pretending to be a skirt
near flags, Venetian, EU, and Turk

exchange near Rialto bridge climbing with angels
from Carmelite monks to thick barbarians' skulls

Bridge of Sighs prisoners paused over watery state
souvenir carts canopy dogs panting in the shade

jester masks and peddled goods in dappled sunshine
sparkled eyes spooky and macabre, even in daytime

Mary at the Pantheon

Only Mary can make me kneel
galvanized in heavenly halo
of soft electric lights

to get just the right angle
of her graceful watch over three
tousled new moon Roman children

their fingers flicker, point, and needle
tea candle flames, starfish of ocean
tapestry's dome and textile triangles

antiquity in transcendence, gilt age
granite columns guffaw, giant elephant
legs trample down from Roman heavens

pagan clouds thunder the piazza, rouse
archaic, dusty gods who snake narrow
alleyways until an unmoved Stoic

Triton trumpets his conch shell
in strident siren, yet it is Santa Maria
who arches my knees into genuflect

After the Vatican Staircase Photo was Developed

lens dust particles
           hovering Catholic orbs
                inquisitive circles appeared
           once liquid poured down film
Papal, spectral, spiral

Train Passengers

On the train to Florence
    a Papa Bear Tony   Soprano
type hoists my backpack

above our heads
    into the luggage rack
Grazie, I say,
    he shrugs,   reveals
a gentle crooked   smile
so endearing, I fight an urge
    to take his hand in mine

soon distracted
    by a sophisticated   woman
sitting across from us
Victoria Beckham's
    Italian twin
-insert Oregano Spice joke-

    wrapped in thigh   high
leather boots, skinny
jeans, black, of course
    fancy leather belt lush
like her, polished, posh
    with Prada bag

pointed elbows pressed
against a nun in full   habit
    bowing her holy head
to the thick, cool window
    next to a faux   blonde

flipping through a glossy
magazine, *Wild Sex!*   splashed
   in lemon yellow font
across its slick cover

A.M. Hayden   49

When you said "No" to Seeing the David

(A Pantoum for Douchebags)

When you said "no" to seeing the David
you missed his fervent magnetic pull of your psyche
to colossal, veined hands so human in God's favor
dozens of incomplete creations wrestling to be freed

you missed his fervent magnetic pull of your psyche
three years' gestation, reveal from one marble block
dozens of incomplete creations wrestling to be freed
artists before tried, failed, declared it *insufferable*

three years' gestation, reveal from one marble block
Firenze brick by brick barrier for three years of war
artists before tried, failed, declared it *insufferable*
like you, who could not be trusted to any wonder

Firenze brick by brick barrier for three years of war
to colossal, veined hands so human in God's favor
like you, who could not be trusted to any wonder
when you said "no" to seeing the David

School of Athens (an Ode to Philosophy)

Frescoes, not paint at all, not surface coated, instead colors mixed into clammy plaster, *fresh* images birthing the wall itself, landscape, institution, Pope's library, thin paper volumes, the rope is pulled open and I walk into the slight room with theater screen sized paintings, a Vatican Grand Canyon I want to climb, backpack, donkey ride into, walk up to Plato and Aristotle center stage with their otherworldly/worldly yin and yang tomes

Heraclitus's fire and flux impermanence, you can't step in the same river twice, Pythagoras and his vegan harmony of spheres, immortal souls, women as equals, but only in his pocket, not in the astronomer's corner of Ptolemy and Zoroaster, where Raphael himself is antisocial artist, awkward in any setting, desperately looking for a dog to pet, exiled Diogenes laying on the steps below, barking with brutal honesty, *there's nothing shameful about being human!*

Mojo Risin' of vintage philosophy in stank tatters instead of leathers, growling *you're blocking my light!* to Alexander the Great, agreeing with Socrates, happiness cannot be bought, speaking of, there he is, gadfly taunting question after ironic question as truth's midwife, offense burning their faces, his sworn, cave-emerged duty to examine and escape, if only Nietzsche, Sartre, or Beauvoir were here, but not a cynical glimmer yet in 1511, maybe a 20th century Hopper version of *Nighthawks,* angsty

arguments, *Je ne sais quoi* stirring in their cigarette smoke, and I can never teach Kierkegaard without thinking of that one student who swore, *If I would have met Kierkegaard, I would have said, don't ever let go of what you love, you dumbass!* referring to Regina, but everything else too and Plato looks like Leonardo, pointing to metaphysical forms of *Good*, no one can teach us anything that is not already buried somewhere inside of us waiting to be unearthed, Gibran said this too, so there must be something to this theory of birth trauma shaking all knowledge to the ground, a loose sack of change turned upside down, spending our whole lives picking up the pieces, which is exactly where Aristotle points to truth, your feet in the dirt, don't miss the real forms by staring at Plato's Sun, and there is patient Hypatia, Neo-Platonic Smurfette of Athens, only one besides Raphael who looks directly at us, wonders where Clea, Thecla, Sosipatra, Diotima Macrina, and the thousands of other unnamed

but *brilliant* word-filled women are at, Hypatia knew she would be blamed for a male ruler's actions, could she have known she would be torn apart literally dismembered piece by piece by an angry Christian mob in the street, and I think it was Socrates who said an educated person is defined by their ability to entertain an idea *without agreeing to it* and 2500 years later, we still look at those who climb out of the cave, dirt crusted under their nails, in fearful disgust, offense burning our faces

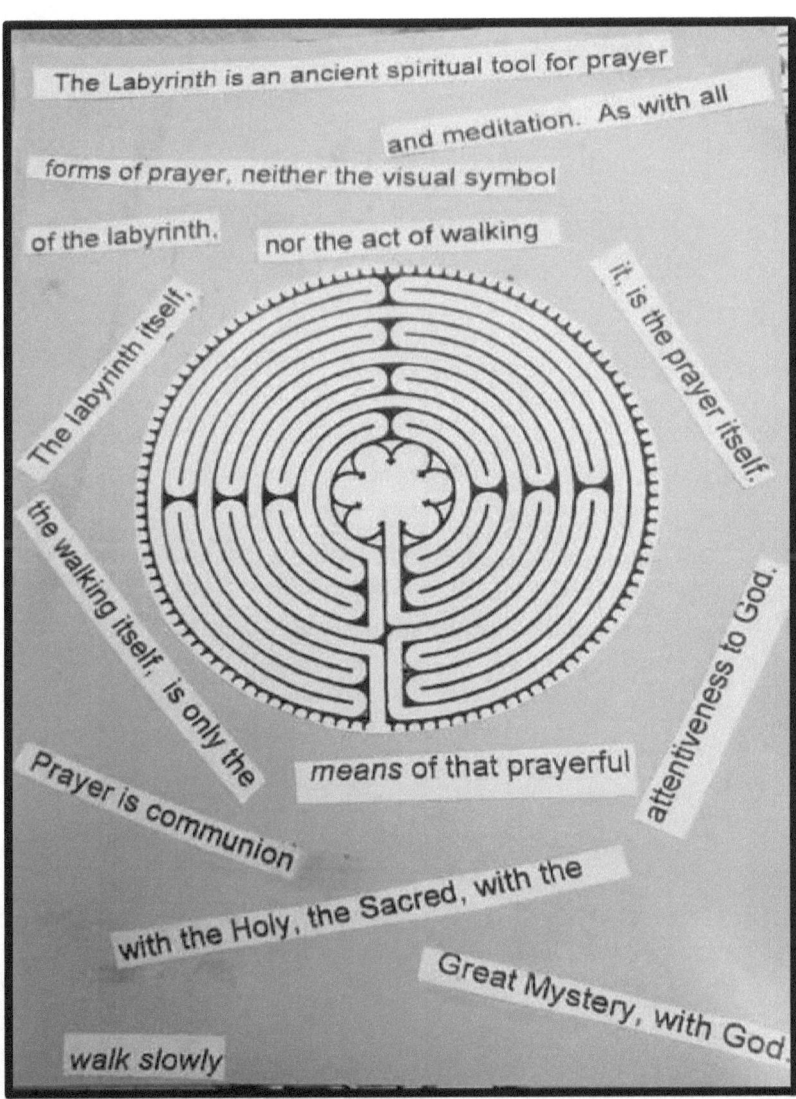

The Labyrinth is an ancient spiritual tool for prayer and meditation. As with all forms of prayer, neither the visual symbol of the labyrinth, nor the act of walking it, is the prayer itself. The labyrinth itself, the walking itself, is only the means of that prayerful attentiveness to God. Prayer is communion with the Holy, the Sacred, with the Great Mystery, with God.

walk slowly

FRANCE

(Paris and Versailles)

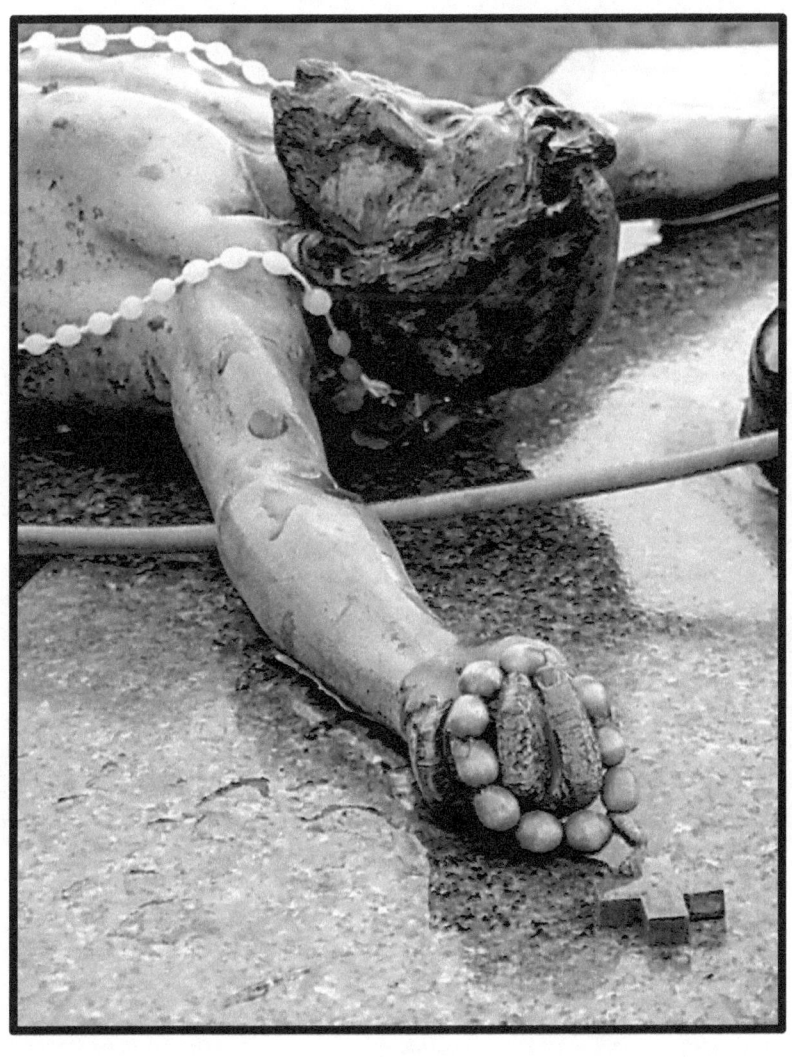

How to Find Jim Morrison's Grave

Squirming Toad
Stop. Enter gates of Paris' *grandest address*
Sweep awe and reverence, tongue over vision
Say prayers for peace frogs, spirits of winter leaves
Choose a path, beautiful friend
Notice odd tombs, doors crooked teeth in a giant's mouth
scattered in uneven rows and mausoleums
Lean your face over after you are called over
Look way down into the blackness, limitless, free
Feel an eerie shiver climb up your spine
Jump back and shudder, attempting to shake it off
even if one is afterlife ambivalent, it is wise
to know when to back off

Love Street
Meander labyrinth of confusing cobblestone
Cut past Heloise and Abelard, monk bought lunch
star crossed lovers with elaborate plans
Flirt with Oscar Wilde as everyone does, evident
in lipstick kisses and tucked, I dare you love notes
lone fuzzy maroon glove delicate on the soaked marble
Tell yourself you must be getting closer, while the famous
dead are fascinating, any American tourist worth their salt
knows there is one reason to visit Père Lachaise

Highway West
Turn again, past the weeping statues
Sigh in relief when you see petite, printed graffiti *"Jim"*
next to a tiny heart next to pointed arrow
driver, where you taking us?
Take another right until you see Jim's headstone
Realize immediately it is not his, the modest one

away from this main corridor hidden from view,
in between other graves like row houses, that's Jim

Gold Mine
Eye the single red roses with orange edged petals
filling the hunkered rectangle plot, their bloomed
wet faces pressed like devoted, curious children
listening through their parents' door, skinny legs
wrapped in watery plastic, romantic Italian bust
stolen years ago, contraband in some French or Austrian
closet or attic, existing now only in a picture
like his lion's youth, one stocky rectangle marker remains:
                    James Douglas Morrison 1943-1971

Ancient Lake
neighboring graves Pollock-splashed with graffiti
Long Live the Lizard King!
Mr. Mojo Risin
Ride the snake
Break on through
This is not the end, Jim!

Seven Miles
Recall the exact moment you knew escape
13-years-old, neighbor's basement floor,
after she, two years older, rifles
through her Dad's stack, slides a stiff record
out if its crinkled sleeve

Petition
Pull off your Walkman headphones full of Queen of Pop
confetti notes as a driving drum pulse explodes from needle
to speaker, lifts you up, feet and legs dangling, arms pinched
to sides, blast off or gripped in a fist, don't know, don't care
as you dip into islands and eyes, chains, lies and Brazilian basslines

sight fuzzed, thoughts melting, an amusement park
scrambler ride, slung corner to corner
in some beautiful, deliberate, geometric pattern

until everything stops, rocket fist drops
to whispered turntable scratch, your lit candle
never snuffed after that, every album, every lyric
even *The Soft Parade* held you in its wacky niche
through the punishing purgatory of middle school
a carnival of prose, conjured ceremony and power
first breakthrough of what poetry can do

Prayer
Look up as it begins to mist over the tombs
like a film noir, gaze back to the graffiti
Note the absence of *"No one here gets out alive"*
such a missed opportunity

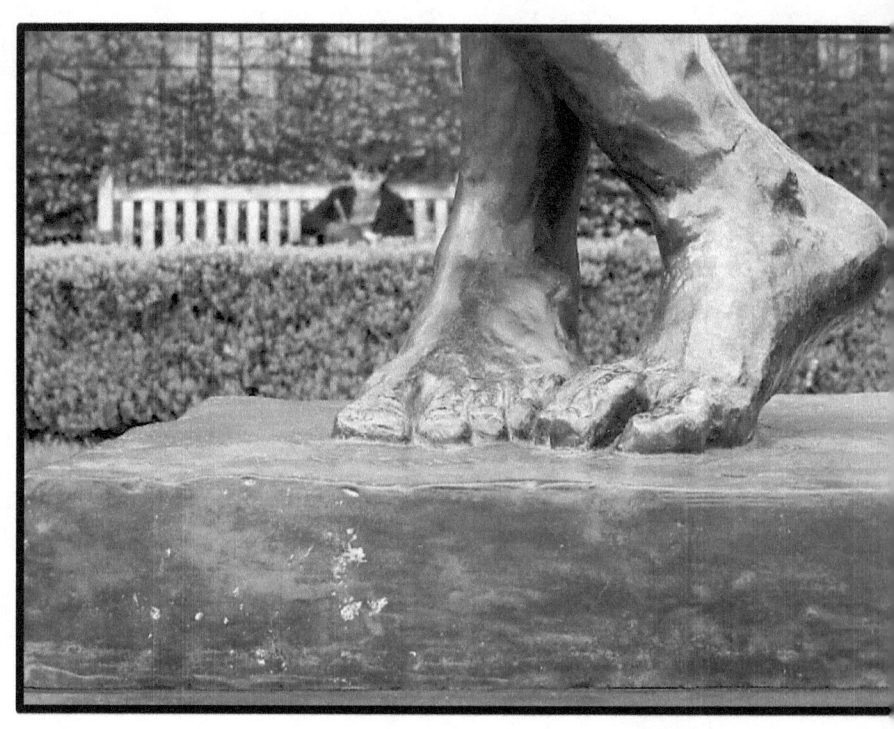

Hemingway

This chic café that once served pigeon killers
       with no heat, no food in their rooms
now charges 12 euros a cup,
       starving artists always manage
to find cigarettes and coffee
       even in the Luxembourg gardens

64   Old World Wings

Sparkles

a magic tower, sensational tower, enlightened light
    on its feet tower
an iconic tower, iron skeleton tower, a French fry fingertip
    gripping glimmer tower
a needle nose looks through a telescope tower
a gaze down below to the sparkling galaxy of twinkling stars
    tinsel tower
a perfectly great expectation thought-they-would-propose-
    but-they-didn't tower
a-long-ride-back-down-after-disappointment tower,
    1889 World Expedition Liberty Sister tower
to Americans - a romance sequins tower
to Parisians - a gaudy lamp post tower, *silly Americans*
scrawled names and graffiti messages in the tiny bathroom
at the top of the tower, in magic marker,
    "I left my poop in the Eiffel Tower!"
smiley face emoji right after this declaration tower
tallest structure for miles, perfect antenna tower
    is the only reason it wasn't torn down tower
a don't you dare jump off this tower
a famous scientologist who jumped on a couch
proposed on this tower, lit-up magic mission
    nearly impossible rocket splendor tower
7,000 tons of bedazzled stretched stars shimmering
from earth to sky tower, golden hour, sour glower,
    flower power, our flashing wower tower

Arrondissements

She is a pulsing
afterbirth, sundry albums
of scrapbook cities

Café de Flore

And *Les Deux Magots*
both places, spaces
lingering with Simone's
smoke and sighs
decided existential intuition
thousands of pushback pages
opposing othering,
insisting "one is not born
yet becomes a woman"
gender a social construct
she declared in 1949
and last year my daughter
was a doctor for Halloween
her cousin as well
same cold stethoscopes
same thin white coats
at each candy stop with buckets out
"what a handsome doctor you are" to him
"what a sweet nurse you are" to her
she loves dinosaurs too
and I hunt for them in the gloomy blue
and grey sections alongside race cars
and "lock up your daughters" onesies
because science is for boys according
to ubiquitous pink unicorn pajamas
like Beauvoir pulled off shelves

pearl clutched *pornography*
herself a child who once yearned
to be a nun until her priest's
broken betrayal led her to find holy
solace in mahogany bars, dim
night's women, furs and violets,
in crisis of faith, Denis, who lit
Marguerite's cigarettes
her radical authentic flame ignited

Size doesn't Matter (Mona Lisa)

women were not painted this way, in this pose
did not hold our bizarre gaze, openly shrewd
no jewels, no crowns, only delicate brush strokes

renaissance sorceress holding our fixed view
chiaroscuro in velvet shade, rebirthed light
muscle movement nuances in soft sinew

her artist's hands peeled cold cadavers at night
discovered in the deep layers how we see
300 years later, she still charms our sight

whispered eros eyelash layers of intrigue
spellbound by her quivering lip mystery

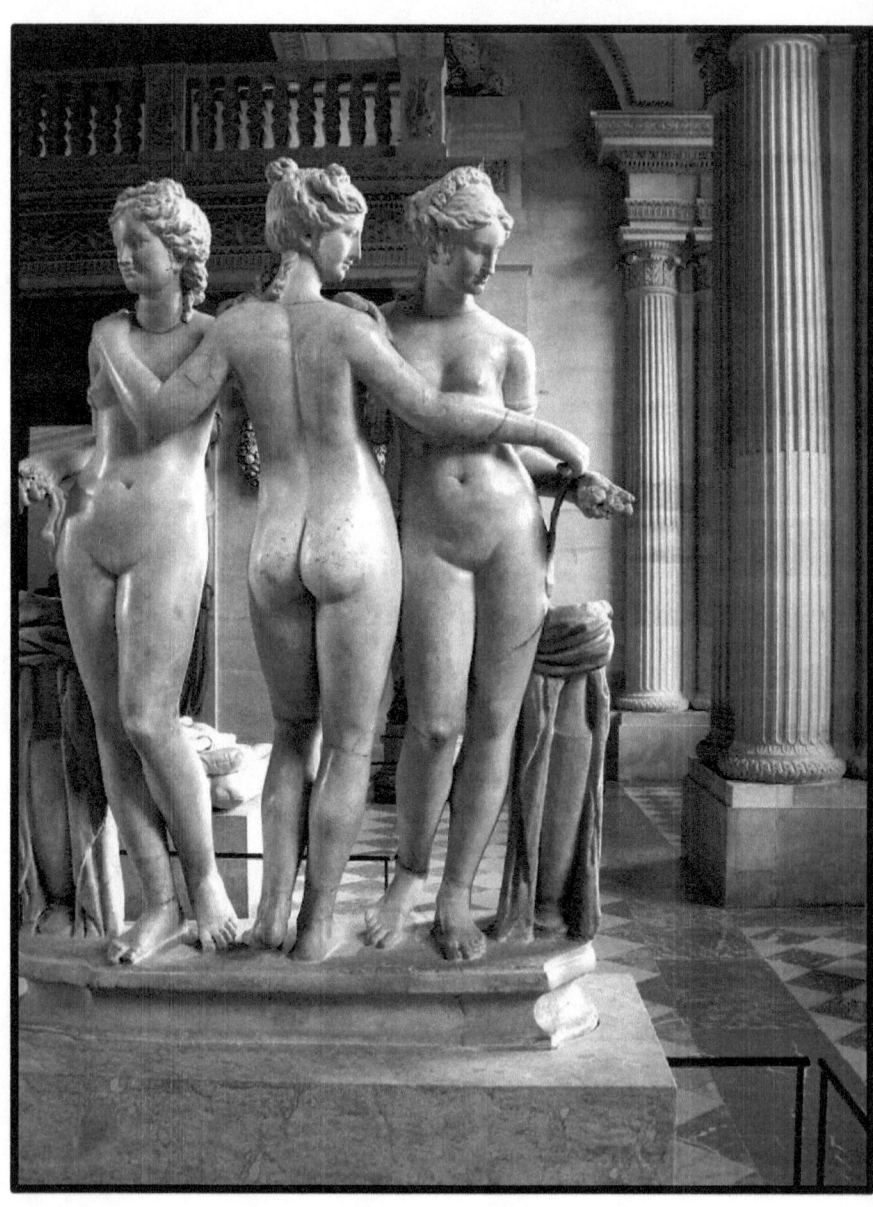

Louvre Fem

soft bellies, slick breasts
snake slithered around her neck
swerve swirl of curls

76　Old World Wings

Musée Érotique Villanelle

Religion and sex together may be hard to grasp
So be sure to see all seven floors
If you visit the sex museum after Mass

A 6' Mesopotamian pottery penis, painted crevasse
No need for privacy, confessionals, or closed doors
Religion and sex together may be hard to grasp

Some may think it titillating, others will find it crass
Either way, you will likely want to see more
If you visit the sex museum after Mass

While a *"Garden of Need"* may not warrant a pass
Will erotic postcards with nuns dressed as whores?
Religion and sex together may be hard to grasp

Or what about S&M priests in leather face masks?
You may be offended, but never bored
If you visit the sex museum after Mass

Nude statues or naked photographs behind glass?
One person's art is another's blushed porn
And all a stone's throw from Montparnasse
If you visit the sex museum after Mass

Umbrellas and Crosses

No thunderstorms here in Paris
　　　　　just mist, just biting wind chill
steep climb to rounded Sacré Cœur, domed
　　　　　Cathedral, Knighted Castle
sword-whipped Parisian cake, stretched sweet
　　　　　candied arches, perpetual prayers rising
as cold rain drips down, long slick fingers
　　　　　blanket of opened umbrellas
hazy blue, gray, black, somber shades of Good
　　　　　Friday, one bright neon orange floral
yellow splash shouting, *I didn't get the memo*
　　　　　or *I'm a tourist from Florida*
or *I will belong on Sunday's rejoicing!*
　　　　　No matter, the colors cry out
to the black-robed Abbott heaving the 10-foot
　　　　　wooden cross, its heaviness
a lifeless body over the rough fabric of his right
　　　　　shoulder while another uses
both hands to grip its length while a third
　　　　　raises a black umbrella
over his vulnerable head or maybe they
　　　　　are carrying a reclining buddha
who is in on the whole thing, laughing

   dozens of smaller crosses raised up

above the umbrella sea against silhouettes

   of the bare March trees

un-bloomed in this early holy week

   looking like wrought iron waiting

patiently for their glorious resurrection

   into spring scent of prayer incense

mythos moored sacred steps

   stay slick underneath soles

where all of us pray in French

   and everything is damp holiness

Hugging Nun

you can tell by the way they are dressed
and by the history clinging to their soaked lips
floors slick with stomps of rain boots and snapping
shut of pointed umbrellas, sable coats sprayed
with droplets, unrequested baptisms, faces with closed
eyes and open mouths, kneeling every direction, candle-lit
prayers caressing saint statues' frozen feet, genuflecting
since womb's holy waters, since Joan of Arc charged
with her 4th century sword, since pagan ancestors invoked
under crone tree canopies as a smiling, plump nun
beams like morning light lifts the horizon

you can tell by the way she is dressed
and by the herstory cradled between her vowed lips
and rosehip cheeks and you have a sudden splendid urge
to reach out your sodden hands for her robed, powder soft
French arms to hold you like she is Amma, the Indian
hugging saint, but you remember the French
are often more kissers than huggers, no thunderstorms
either, mostly just misting like London,
like Seattle, just hug-less damp dreaming

Cottage Core Hamlet (Marie I)

17th century slow living fantasies
        Her Queen's "Rustic" Retreat
puffed sleeves at ease, long legume flutes
        little lambs in the meadow
grazing greener grass, softened shoes,
        ribbons, sunhats, peaceful splash
of geese, Francois frogs, of *Hameau de le Reine*
        open windows, curtain breeze
eggs prewashed by the servants,
        farm sanitized for comfort
while Marie and her maidens drank sweet
        goat milk from fine flowered porcelain
plucked glossiest eggs from dry nesting boxes
        after all, one can hardly imagine her
mucking out a musky goat pen, or cleaning
        a coop splattered with rooster shat
it was mostly magic and wildflowers for her
        even royalty tire of their gilded artifice
long to pluck their own strawberries, taste
        juicy seeded red flesh on their tongues

Montmartre Mischief

Crème brûlée   fetish gnome
       fantasy's roam   cherry earrings
dangling polaroids rapid heartbeat
       photo booth   grain sacks
hilly mystery   spring afternoons
       sneezed dust   paper scraps
skipped stones   bisous delight

Latin Quarter Cabaret

If France is a lady, Paris is the bedsheet
entangled pantaloons, pocketknife's electric sleep
pointed triangle couture, liquid exhaustion
sharpshooter wisdom, antique ghost haunted
moxie street performers, busking musicians
carts of kitschy blinking Eiffel keychains
hipsters breakdancing on cobblestones of Seine
playing U2's *Desire,* we sing as loud as we can
children in easter hats, colors of poofed fruit
pop black and white backdrop, rats, and racoons,
racial conflict, erotica, and hijab rights, armfuls
of bleu cheese and baguettes carried on bikes
commuters stepping over a man passed out cold
dirty underbelly, squealing echo of metro
fashioned manicured nails chic neon pink glow
sneered shine no coquette pigeon can smoke

Now I See (Notre Dame before the Fire)

Now I see why farmers and peasants
dropped to their dusted knees
shadowed pilgrims through fishnet partitions
kaleidoscope glass, blurry apparitions in prism
geometric galaxies, choir unleashing chariot
songs and celestial trumpets
is this what the Rose Window
would sound like when it sings?
shard colors rising like incense, like heat,
swirling, burning otherworldly wonder
Mary's elongated arms reaching out to us
in embers, under Goliath's exemplar cross
could she know what she signed up for forever?
did Socrates, when he clawed out of the cave?
meticulous Plato does not mention the dirt
surely burrowed under stiff fingernails
just like illiterate farmers' in the blazing light
blinded and delirious with enlightenment
now kneeling where Crusaders petitioned prior
to igniting their holy wars, heavy history's
combustion engines, bones and sinew, organ
notes hanging in eclipsed post-burn ashen air
what we have lost to humanity's inferno
despite our desperate attempts
to preserve every written page

Gargoyles I

creep up each millennium spiral stair
curled in conch shell, clenched thousand-year-old fist
catch your breath, eye to stone eye

guardians holding off bad spirits since 1163
with giant open seashell ears that leaked out ocean sky
years ago, horned, muscled and graceful

human hands tapering into pointed Dracula
fingernails, playfully leaning on pointed elbows
both hands slapped onto face *Home Alone* style

claws edge gripped, bird beaked stretch to sky
chipped tooth snapped in half, manmade steeple
stalagmite, pointed ears, turret tongue curled

hooked mouth lick of own curved chest, curtain
heavy eyebrows, menacing canine teeth. others smooth
nubs like St. Peter's rubbed Roman toe

moss covered cement guardians atop every corner
shrouded under scales, wings, and weather's layers
would they alter with a power wash baptism?

round head, gaunt cheekbones like your friend Ben
who got clean six months ago, and *someone took
time to carve a perfect tongue*

now speckled in white tictacs of pigeon poop,
a fugue of *Dark Crystal* puppets cloak-draped
head to claws, exposed toenails every rooftop

French life's layered arches, intricate shapes, detailed lines,
apparition's specks, figurines in shocking teal stepping
out from ash black lampposts

book or staff or knife or fist in the air, ink blot spire
that could be stolen from a medieval vampire
hundreds of profiles punching out from sides

strong forearms with face fists, eyes wide shut
waiting to ascend with the ancients while the boy
far down below in black mittens, back turned

to all of this, watches pigeons flutter, recognizing
small angels showing off their wings, whispering
their vespers to him, *we are holy too*

Gargoyles II

Under fisted faces, sloshy blue eyed
      street performer in red hoodie and blue jeans
      wears a flimsy dime store mask, *troll* mask,

not *gargoyle* for the record, then sneaks around
      the souvenir store to scare unsuspecting
      pedestrians, running up behind them

to pull a scarf, jump scare, a woman shrieks, a man
      shakes his fist, yet nothing dissuades
      this unnerving imp as he creepily mimics

their stride, turns on his heels, most wave
      him away like a swatted fly, some angrily
      curse him, a lone few laugh

he just keeps on going
      what you can get away with
      wearing, and not wearing, a mask

Rodin's Lover

you taste his gruff voice
you drink his stabbing steel eyes
fingers chiseling
you grasp his love letter palms
impressive relief

Wild Nights on Seine

after Emily Dickinson

On rocking boat, slick moon licks our cheeks, wild
serendipity, our Jungian compass of nights -
sweating the sheets into a torrid kind of wild
giddy plunge while the rest row ordinary nights
yet our mouths pulse like hearts as if we were
painted into *Starry Night's* swirl, a Paris I
have been smitten with since I was a girl, with
windy passage, pillow talk ripple, how do I love thee
Paris je t'aime, watch me arch into a lioness wild
under silver bow, luminating dusky knotted nights
sip me like the sweetest port, lap me like a leopard would
you have never been this hungry, you will never be
again after me, futile others oblivious to our
stained glass growls, howling taste of lupine luxury

You're Welcome

Je vous en prie means
You are welcome and also
I will pray for you
which is a quite tender thing
for the waitress or bus boy
to say to you as you leave

Women have always said "Sorry" (Marie II)

Un.
(It is said)
after her graceful walk
all dressed in white
she politely apologized
to her executioner
for stepping
on his foot

Deux.
Hair shocked white
no more need for panache or powder
or Queen's Chocolatier
flour and bread insurrection mob
found her hide and seek filigree
behind her harp and harpsichord

Trois.
Under arched fresco cherub ceilings
stretched by ornate hall of mirrors
her lacquered, painted reflection
every embroidered surface swooped
and poufed, bejeweled and brocaded
flowered and plumed, birdsong flute
chandelier wig of ships

Quatre.
It is easy to forget, before angry peasants
stormed cobblestone streets
before their banging on the Bastille Fortress
before her best friend's head
was pike mounted for her view
her voice carved green geometrics

trimmed trellises, impolite gardens
untightened corsets and milkmaid cottages

Cinq.
and the thrashing horses
spraying wild water
unleashed secret smiles
unbridled masquerade fantasies

Six.
of frosting fabrics, frivolous feathers,
card games and cream champagne,
lip pink strawberries, hushed baby blue
macaron silk fans, jeweled easter garters
lemon yellow candied amusements

Sept.
away from the privileged Queen
they dressed her to be each day
encrusted with charms and chokers
away from the tarnished reputations

Huit.
conjured by 18th century
scandal rags and Paparazzi
smacking her across her cheeks
until they turned into
rotten sardines peeled open

Neuf.
How dare she and her lace,
her diamond and her cake
her hamlet by the lake
how dare a 14-year-old
Austrian girl, whose crooked
teeth and mouth offended,
fixed through jaw bone corset

Dix.
How dare she
and every woman
who recognizes herself
when she steps
on her own executioner's foot
and whispers *Pardon,*
Je suis désolée
I'm sorry

Eastern Europe

(Austria, Czech Republic, Poland)

Sunrise Over Austria

Jagged German mountains striped
      by Sherbert sun-swaths, two flight
attendants clad in red leather, *Guten Morgen,*
      they offer in energetic unison
smile widely, white-blonde hair
      wrapped in baby blue scarves
the shape of tiny x's, cherry leather knee
      boots, nearly vivid as the peaks
blazing behind them through
      the plane's oval window

Vienna Skate Park

click clack, click clack
horse drawn carriage, driver in a top hat
tips the brim, holds my eyes, lips raised
in whispered German secrets
offers a cigarette from his left hand

near the cathedral with the gloriously
pointed steeple, cement walls bathed
in anti-Neo-Nazi flyers, street
graffiti of a barn-red penis, also pointed

stern-faced goddess across the alley
grips a stone wreath in each patina palm
bronzed body slick dolphin skin
I half expect to hear piano quartets

instead, it is the grind of skateboard wheels
slaps of wooden deck hitting the concrete
clack clack, clack clack
Viennese adolescents practicing ollies

What would it be to *grow up* in Vienna?
Same acne, same angst and giant feelings
just beneath the canopy of creaking
14th century bridges, under aloof eyes
of unmoved 17th century composers

unnoticed by the Old-World woman
laboring through the fogged park
with her cane. no matter to the pigeons
shaking out their Old-World wings

Before Sunrise

Was it this green bridge
where they learned about the cow
who smokes with his hooves?

Did they stop fighting
at the restaurant in Greece,
decide they're worth it?

Did they ride a train
for their anniversary,
have sex near the Seine?

Most importantly,
are there any new waltzes,
does she still write songs?

Memento Mori I

mummified monks
underground museum
cloak-and-dagger crypt
sullied scent
graves cellar
crumbling bodies
gray skin
putrefied paper
exposed mandibles
decayed digits
rosary wound
don't want
to look
can't look
away from
brittle silence
their reminder
to remember
still echoes
we are
all dust
and bones

Memento Mori II

As a kid, you put
your tongue-tied
faith in crashing waves
hidden street shadows
of broken vows
You put it in harmful
and violent words
wasted truth, red velvet
trivial tea for two
You put it in adobe
prayers, believers,
forgivers
flesh and bone
pay the price
Now, you put it in
your privileged
crown of silence
lessons learned
a place to sit still
in the snow

*tribute to Depeche Mode

Krampus and Cider

the Ren fair of Brno
ice winded celebration of St. Nick's Day
Orthodox saint with a penchant
for gift giving
and miracles
manifested in a holiday
of colorful fuzz hats and hot cider

three figures on the hayride
young girl in bright white angel robe
hair encircled by halo
alongside the horned devil,
looking more like
Chewbacca and a yeti mated
Bumble with red hanging tongue

more a winter's Gene Simmons
or fuzzy Kali than a medieval Lucifer
running and roaring
to scare children, make them cry
talons poking shirts
and zippers teasing 'til thoroughly
upset, sobbing wet Czech children tears

St. Nick steps in
jolly red and white bearded savior
calms them with candy
and treats, wondering
if the old tales
are all in fun, Krampus
rounding up all the bad children

                    tying them into a sack
throwing them in the river
            like a farmer's
            unwanted kittens
                        or if there is some dark
            truth to why these kids are so
noticeably well behaved

A.M. Hayden   123

Melrose Place Kangaroo

At an Australia bar
        Czech students eat Kangaroo
discuss U.S. politics
they don't blame us, by the way
they ask our majors, our names
        after I say mine
one girl's eyes light up, scooting
closer, "Ooooh, like Melrose Place!"

Brno Bell and Crocodile

You hear the ancient bell
　　　　in center square, the one Napoleon
stood under, reached up on tiptoes to ring
　　　　it is tradition to ring the bell
as you walk through marketplace
　　　　ding dang dong, steady all day

You make a promise to ring
　　　　this bell through blur of bright colors
maroon, magenta, lavender, hot pink,
　　　　the women in short skirts, no tights
bare legs pouring themselves
　　　　into tall boots, Czech or Italian

You shiver against frosted
　　　　December window, sipping
strong coffee in a tiny teacup
　　　　served on a small saucer
an even tinier spoon clanging its side
　　　　warm foggy Fibonacci spiral

You see a woman
　　　　short skirt, no tights
run up to her fully pregnant friend
　　　　drop to her knees to cup her swollen belly
with both palms, covering the surface
　　　　kisses bouncing across on the moon

A.M. Hayden　　127

You think of the crocodile plaster replica
        hanging in the main square
homage to the live crocodile brought to Brno
        five hundred years ago, no one
had ever seen or heard of a crocodile
        so they called him their *dragon*

You smile when you hear they fed him
        and he lived a fat, slow, happy
life in Brno, becoming their beloved mascot
        listening to the bell
ring steady all day long
        ding dang dong

No One Knows Where Mozart is Buried

We search through the maps
Vienna claims they have him
Salzburg insists he
rests with them, our waiter shrugs,
"just let the mystery be"

"Matka Boska 'Karmiaca'"

the first time
     I see   sublime
Mary breastfeeding
her baby   Jesus

I do not feel
     like a   voyeur
the opposite,
as I too am   comforted

fed at her
     round   breast
blood transubstantiating
into milk, into   sanctuary

soft thighs and feet
     chunky   Christ child
beholding His
cobalt-robed   mother

gazing back at him
     in Oxytocin haze
unguarded fullness
I recognize in my daughter's

eyes watching me
     years later   my milk
let down
resuscitating   my faith

*"Matka Boska Karmiaca" is Polish for Our Lady "Breastfeeding" or "Nurturing"

Czech Castles, Krakow Churches

crumbling walkways

13th century pillars

ephemeral ghosts

alone, old European

churches, castles too,

chill to the bone

on last wooden pew

women praying in Polish

grainy voices swirling

incense floating down

bathing faith grappled face

un-communion mouth

whisps curling around

hang to severe kneeling bench

resting on what gives

136   Old World Wings

Orthodox Physical

Achat אַחַת

You rush into Krakow's oldest synagogue, *women to the left, men to the right,* and you knew this was coming, but it is one thing to know and another to be *the one* prohibited, steered up squeaky steps to the boxed, windowless room, wait, one window, a teeny square centered just above your reach, Minecraft eye in opaque brick. You stand on tiptoes, cartoonishly bounce a few pathetic times, spot a swath of wooden wall, a moment of brown ceiling.

Sh'tayeem שְׁתַּיִם

You land, defeated, sit on the long bench behind the wall, it is Friday freaking *Shabbos* and you cannot hear the Torah being read in Hebrew like it has been for centuries, you try not to flounder into serious fomo, strive not to dwell on Brian, who always complains and always wears plaid, complaining, in today's plaid shirt before we entered, "I don't want to go to this stupid church."

Shalosh שָׁלֹשׁ

You sought to unclench your jaw and asked mercy to not to sound like an asshole when you replied tightly, "it's not a church, Brian, this is a synagogue, one of the oldest, one of the most special synagogues. The *only* one here that survived the Nazis." You tried not to say, *it's a big f-ng deal, Brian, this is what perseverance looks like, Brian,* and now you sit in a one-windowed room while Brian and the others with sleepy penises are bathed in warm sunlight filtering through centuries-old windows, front row VIP inner sanctuary grandness, draped in holy bells and smells, hearing sacred Hebrew scripture read from papery thin scrolls a tiny hand-shaped *yad* holds in place.

Arbah אַרְבַּע

You stare at the white bricks of the one-windowed wall, then look over to the women in scarves and wigs holding chumash, staring into the space in front of them, you wonder if they made peace long ago, witnessing their mothers and grandmothers sit on these rigid benches while men below blew shofars, draped tallis, wrapped tefillins, head and heart, did they decide, like the Quakers, simplicity is closer to God, for weathered women whose wombs withered, whose wringed wrists tied brisket, do not need suffer production for Divine intimacy.

Chamaysh חָמֵשׁ

You sit in silence. You begin to pray. You pray some more until the sound of the small door opening turns your sight to a rabbi's waving arm, sign of empty hourglass, impatiently shooing everyone out, you file down the stairs, into the street where Brian moans, "Jesus, that was so boring, so long, *ugh*, where's a bar?" You stare into the space in front of you trying not hit his square face, man's religion, *The Lord, our God, our Lord is One*, but not God, no, because synagogues were used as storehouses for potatoes, because this is one of the holiest places, head and heart, head and heart, only men would pretend it is *God* who cares if you pass their physical.

*menorah (candelabra); shofar (ram's horn); chumash (prayer book); tallis (prayer shawl); tefillin (sacred containers for prayer); yad (silver or wood pointer for the Torah)

Protestant Sympathizer

there in the wall
this one, right in front of you,
a man was cemented alive

a 17th century Catholic
x = heresy, empathy
sealed into an example

history them vs. hearsay us
post-plague, plaque inscription
x marks the spot

Execution Circle Triolet

What a slight circle to swallow such terror
I surmise as I devour my potato pancake, as
I spoon creamy goulash from the market vendor

What a slight circle to swallow such terror
Flat death clock dwarfed by bursting plague pillar
Surviving sun saint rising to touch the landscape

What a slight circle to swallow such terror
I surmise as I devour my potato pancake

The rest of the poems in this Eastern European section feature themes, history, and stories of the Holocaust, including Auschwitz.

Please read with care.

This Art Student's Apartment

was gentrified from a Nazi Ghetto
still crumbling bricks,
glass, and tires turned trendy,
a renovated place to reside

I want to ask her, *but how
can you* live *here?*
Live in the echoes of such fear?
she offers us a tour, same structure

hobbit hole without cottage
core cheer, a stylish basement
cave, an abyss in the middle
of her living room floor, a glass

covered tunnel, you can stand
right on top of it, peer down
into unending obscurity,
how many climbed through this?

one on top of the other, I wonder,
thinking of her eating toast and tea
watching reality tv, next to this giant
black hole, full of quiet ghost mouths wide open

"Lovey"

after the boycotts
after the Professor firing
after the book burning
after the street beatings
after rounding up families
separated by the river
patrolled and gated

only one family escaped
these claustrophobic tunnels
the wealthy shoemaker
because even in a holocaust
money speaks, at least it did
here in this dismal maze
of crumbled bricks, old tires
and broken glass, a half-torn
stuffed bear left behind

150 Old World Wings

Roma Museum

Never the Egyptians they are mistaken for,
never a ~~g*psy~~ slur, but "the people"
       the *Romani* with Indo-Aryan veins
filled with   folklore, paramecia and fingers
that flicker accordions, violins,   cellos
     with   rounded feet and spinning wheels
of a hundred languages, dialects, religions
here   in this   place
they are Czech-Sanskrit speaking
eclectic Hindu Catholics   praying
     to home altars, in colorful headscarves
each floor of this museum dripping
with documents, display boxes, harmonicas,
old violins, music   filling the rooms
escaping overhead speakers
Balkan, Austrian Hungarian, "~~G*psy~~ Punk"
     the guide clarifies
when we notice one raucous song
photographs, one a fortune teller
boldly reading the   palm
of her arresting officer, cigarette dangling
out her puckered mouth, turning to   ash
     they hated   being cooped   up
the government took the wheels off their carts
clipped their   wings
     notorious for breaking the windows,
the Czech guide informs
     centuries of movement escape Spanish enslavement
the *Great Round Up* of   1749
        rounded again in 200 years
to the camps alongside Jehovah's Witnesses, political
     rebels, LGBTQ+   and 6 million Jews

A.M. Hayden   151

Romani women forcibly   sterilized
in *Block 11*, systematic population prevention
      250,000 Roma
         turned to ash
one violin note uncurls a woman's wavering
voice that machete cuts the lower half of a body
      and my knees   buckle
I drop to a bench, don't understand anything
she is saying
         Czech? Russian? Polish?
My insides sliced   open
      I want to howl at the guide standing
over me, instead, I ask, "What *is* this?"
         he nods, "a mother, she sings
for her dead children,
         the ones taken"
250,000 Roma thrown to the fire
Romani phoenixes   escaping
to the next lands, wings washed
         in brilliant-colored feathers
           flickering strings coated
in ashless bells
      and clanging   cymbals

154   Old World Wings

Yellow Fish Sign

bright yellow sign
      carp fish morph
star of David
      jagged grave stones
giant granite mosaic
      cemetery path winds

googly eyes
      lashed lies
sunny and cheerful
      children's crayons
coloring death rites
      inside the lines

156   Old World Wings

Zuzanna

her parents vanished, forced yellow star
mammoth on her frame, spared skinny knees
every child seized. arms that lifted away,
arms that kept them hidden

smile lifts wizened eyes, eyes have seen
what can't be described, she walks us through
Hebrew inscribed rock-lined gravestones
each one storing their story

too many to tell in the time of one brief
guided tour, do the spirits scramble
in expectation on the days it's their turn?
do they rise when they hear their tale told?

like when Nazis hijacked several thousand
men from this village, only ten returned
forearms tattooed with numbers
and Nazis auctioned off

these same Jewish gravestones for profit, stretched
backs still etched with numbers, numbers, numbers

Mitzvah Rocks

some are uneven
to deter grave robbers
some are smooth pebbles
to hold spirit down
until resurrection day
lined observantly
every stone a prayer
permanent visitation
faithful vow to remember
unyielding, unlike
fragile, fleeting flowers

*Mitzvah – "Commandment"

"In Work You Shall Be Free"

Arbeit macht frei
shudders as we walk under
sharp barbed wire gate
of Prisoner's Camp

Arbeit macht frei
Let us, you, and I,
breathe out and in
breathe for each one

Arbeit macht frei
it may not matter
doesn't matter
does it matter?

Arbeit macht frei
there must be
some pause, some
owed recognition

Arbeit macht frei
nothing can explain
what it is to breathe
knowing *we* can leave

Creepy Trees

I

I cannot walk	-	any closer
I cannot shake	-	choking alarm grip
my feet frozen	-	damp earth below
petals and notes	-	tucked in edges
pressed in rocks	-	execution wall
even the trees	-	absorbed unspeakable
sorrow and shrieks	-	layered in rings
gnarled roots	-	crooked branches
hunched leaves	-	silent witnesses
disturbed whispers	-	as you walk by

Bound and Gagged

bouquets

    lay   across the railroad tracks

        the same tracks   that

    transported   people

loaded trains   frightened

    huddled   terrified

    the sight   of this place

    for the first   time

how many knew

    how many screamed

    internally

    visions of fire

and fire   and   fire

    and all   aboard

    yelled,   "Shut Up!"

because how   could they

    believe   it?

    believe   they were   on a train

    to a   death   factory

Earth, Do Not Cover Their Blood

barracks
watchtowers

      miles
          of chimneys

                 textbooks
                 speak
                 sometimes
                    of them

     but not
         how many

                 what eighth
                 grade
                 table insert
                   teaches

    how burning
        in bulk

                 saved Nazi
                 money
                 making it
                   endlessly

                         snow

Block 11

I have to remind myself this is not
a movie set, this is the actual *Death Block*

these brick walls that ricocheted
screams of gynecological experiments

torture, forced open Fallopian tubes
shot up with burning chemicals

brutal mass sterilizations
painful radiation, severe burns

festering sores, fever
hemorrhaging, sepsis

memories of their horrors persist
but not of the women they were before this

Franceska

is her name most think, a Jewish ballerina from Poland
one of millions of daughters, mothers, sisters, girls
huddled, frightened, one of millions
forced to undress in front of nazi soldiers

but museums don't speak of how periods also perished
blood everywhere except for lunar cycles, not only
because of dehydration, malnourishment, but the poisons
injected into their female bodies for "research"

the beatings and rapes by officers, forced pregnancy
terminations following, and the babies allowed
to be born had nothing to suckle, no milk
in their mother's breasts, no milk

and one experiment measured how long a newborn
could survive without its mother's milk -
several days it turns out, until a female Czech doctor
couldn't take the mother's suffering

handed her a syringe full of morphine to end the cries
and the women liked to tell stories of dishes they cooked
before all of this, delicious blintzes and cakes
so many stories of resistance, of the women

who wouldn't leave their children
who followed them into the gas chambers
ensuring their babies wouldn't be alone
for their last breaths

resistance in seams ripped out of German coats,
though women workers tended to slip
handwritten notes in the pockets designed
for women customers, with a direct message

of the gassings, paper to fingertips to thread
to Zyklon B canisters to a Hungarian revolt
that blew up one of the crematoriums, an uprising
that killed several S.S. officers, and it isn't surprising

that women were the ones who supplied
gunpowder, smuggling in small bits
on their bodies and wrapped in cloths, Esther, Ella,
Regina, Róza…and Franceska

who some say used her very essence to resist
she danced, danced to distract the officers,
and when forced to undress, she threw her clothes
in an officer's face, pummeled him with her shoe's heel

then grabbed his gun, shot him and another,
rumors of noses torn half off; hairlines scalped
by grip of women's ferocity, what made her
be one who could not wait, tenacious defiance

what did she and the other women hear
at that moment before the rage -
a sparrow's sing, wind's howl, boot heel's
crunch, the silence that hung in bitter air

what woman could deny this moxie
to go out fighting, and even today when
you walk near the gas chambers left behind
you can hear the birds chirping

Fertilizer

We walk
  the biggest
    cemetery
      of Eastern
        Europe,
          organized,
            systematic,
              staggering
              frugality,
                muffled
                  blanket
                    of whistling
                      December
                      wind.
                        When I
                          ask what
                            Nazis did
                              with all
                                the ashes,
                                  our guide
                                  replies,
                                    "We're
                                      walking
                                        on
                                          them."

176   Old World Wings

Why Witness

Why any of this when you can never articulate it? Because this building, this open room where human beings were shoved, undressed, shaved, taunted, humiliated, windows filtering afternoon light into cruel illusion of warmth, these stories must be spoken

Why even visit a genocide museum? Because the suitcase they had been told to fill, stuffed with tangible evidence of their previous life, confiscated to a vault called *Canada*, "freedom," these stories must be spoken

Why take photographs when you can never capture it? Because this wall to wall stretch of pictures collected from suitcases and satchels, black and white, sepia, colorized, families, grandparents, children sitting on laps, kids playing at the beach in the sand, lovers holding hands, weddings, vacations, school photos, real faces smiling, real lives lived in dream imagery, thousands of snapshots of stories that must be spoken

Why write when you can never explain it? Because we need any sliver of human dignity, a vain attempt to make sense of what is utterly senseless, you stand still in front of these glass rooms, bewildered by towering piles of picture frames, banged pots and pans, rusted kitchen tools, lace-less crackle shoes, bent eyeglass frames, and mounds of razored hair, stacks of parts and possessions, annihilation organized, labeled, curated, and displayed, and if you have never peered through this thin glass while hushed voices around you whisper, *unbelievable,* and *oh my,* and *just horrid,* then, someone must tell it to you, these stories must be spoken

A.M. Hayden   177

When I asked the Holocaust Survivor

"How can you not lose
your faith in humanity
after bearing this?"

His name was Felix,
his response to my question,
I'll never forget.

He calmly replied,
"I trust, but trust with caution,
best advice I've got."

IRELAND

(Donegal and Ireland's Northwest Region)

Author's Note: "faery" is an English version of the Irish "sídhe" (pronounced "shee"). While both are often used interchangeably, the author acknowledges "sídhe" as the most accurate, direct name.

A Waterfall Song

After Yeats' "Drinking Song"

river ribbons, rainbow
colors arch, no doubt thick
moss holds soggy truths, grows
green paths, stones tell whispered
stories, I lift my palms to the trees
faery folklore canopies

Ogham

Pagan pre-Christian communication
Shared stone stories of sixteen centuries
Latin relation, clann situation

Smooth squints face sun's rising east
etches of lines, claw marks, thin grooves precise
piano's black keys, a comb's missing teeth

Chieftain's tenacious notches, four by five
limestone letter, arduous alchemy
brawny shoulder storytellers of time

Bewitching message, sunwise sorcery
Ogham antenna of tongue's spent ages
5th century Gaelic "Remember Me"

Druid Salmon

spoken into fork
and spoon bent trees
shared in bark and leaves
held prayers, poems, stories
pinecone pages bound
in hard husk covers,
until they ungrasp
their branches, plunge
into salmon-filled rivers
where fish grow thick,
layers cracking open shells
ingesting rogue
forest knowledge
netted by human
snared by bear
both now guts deep
in druid wisdom

Sligo Bookstore near Yeats' house

aqua blue doorframes sew borders
around the tiny book market closet,
creaky stairs, book nook diorama
complete with ginger sleeved vinyl
dusty cobweb shelves, small towers
of adventures winding to my shoulders,
paper air, paper nostrils, paper lungs
and a smiling, skinny store owner
who piles one thin sliced poetry book
on top of another in my upturned hands,
mound of mattress pages filled with peas
like *magpie, meadowsweet,*
drumlin, trawl, windbitten,
boondock, buttonhole, sliotar
paper words beanstalk stacked
and I close my eyes
until I am a tower too
until I am ink and wood's dust
swirling up squeaking stairs
a cobweb curiosity
settling in Sligo sunlight

drumlin – small hills
boondock – remote, isolated area
sliotar – ancient hurling ball

I would ask the Grains that Grew

three Millenia after they were planted

when was the moment you knew?
which decade, which century,
which millennia, how many times

did you hesitate, *no, not yet,*
was it an eternity of nothing
until just one bursting instant

or was it magic preserved
steadily alchemized in your abandoned
medieval garden near the sarcophagus?

what was the moment you clambered
through copious layers of Celtic soil
birthing into world unrecognized?

or was it just the same as it ever was

The Winds of Cavan Burren

gusts buttercups and rockrose
carves shamrock carpet
curls through clover and cowslips
340-million-year limestone narrative
whistles the same now as it did then
or does it, what can't be known

feel boggy green yin of earth
give beneath your feet, stone age sinkholes
close your eyes in the ceremony
led by the fiery headed one
slip off your shoes and be reborn as a willow
swaying, praying, decaying

rosette rocks cupped like spotted leopards
moss licking its fuzzy lipped boulder tombs
mouths open, eternal hunger or tropical sea thirst
rocks on top of rocks on top of rocks
like rising dough, shape shifters in invisible cloaks
birth, descent, rebirth stones, sheen of all meaning

peer into the green iris of this moss giant
black pupil a scrying mirror
get wind of which oak is the druid one
staff lightning struck crooked over coltsfoot
slipped among groves of sleek arrows
tipped by shaggy paintbrushes, stand in stillness
at the tomb-turned cattle shed
Boireann blanketed, stand still, again, to feel
dew drops of the wet willow brush your cheek
baptizing you with good fortune, *shh, listen,*
do you heed the sídhes' summon?

Boireann – rocky place/landscape

The Wishing Chair

I sought a Wishing Chair
a royal greensward square
forged boulder throne
pixie path of winding coins
silken tangles conjured
sea spray churned
drenched fishing line petrified
wildflowers amethyst aligned
standing windy
to shining silver tide

196   Old World Wings

Baby Blue Poetry Jukebox

it's quite a surprise   in the stone walls of Derry
                    to find a jukebox
            that plays only poetry
                step   inside, turn the handle
azure spoken word   of joy
            after years
                    of cannon fire

Spitfire Paddy

it's his almost smirk
hawk curved ears
fighter jet lover
whose eyes taxi you up
he, the cool handed boyfriend
the one who would write you lust letters
the one you would never hear from again

200   Old World Wings

Epic Immigration Abecedarian

Arrival! cracked rearview mirror reflections
Brought millions out, abandoning homes, no other
Choice than to seek new life, new land, to
Discover *anywhere* one could survive, could
Eat foreign foods, to adapt to an alien life after
Famine, wild geese flight, fill dance halls, music is
"Good" if "it makes you want to get up and dance"
Haydens who emigrated, how many to seek better
I imagine them in love, hats in hands, dancing
Jigs to horns, grim burdens to floors, like Billy the
Kid did to protect the cattle, orphaned translator
Leave their Eire they had to, but *never* being Irish
Mountain music fused into Appalachian treasures
Nights balmy with banjos, folk songs, stomping and
O'Leary's cow did *not* start that fire, third grade lies
Persecuted her whole life, like so many others
Quiet in their camouflage, if need be, if necessary
Regrets are a waste, instead forged into blazing
Stories of coffin ships, salt water, and epics like the
Táin, cattle raid, singsongs for cursed sleepy men of
Ulster, thick and tenacious, rightful armor for racist
Venom shot from every angle and street corner
Wars in alleys, fights for their mothers' good name
(XP) *Chi Rho* Christos, stigmata, pulp pounded
Yet 70 million of us yearn a dogged lineage beyond
Zombie by Cranberries, galaxies more
                 than green beer on St. Patrick's Day

A Conversation with Queen Maeve

She beckons autumn into blush swirl, seduces revenge's rule,
conquers as Queen of Connacht, curses Ulster's cruelest men,
stricken immobile with viscous childbirth, to avenge

Macha, moaning in their collective misery, her intoxicating
marvel exhaled in Eire's chiseled coastlines and churning foam,
thunder and lightning crackling megalithic mound to sky

in mountains vulva shaped, ruthless or simply fed-up
she *who lets the soft animal of herself love what she loves*
strong cackle, head heaved back, her scoffs vault across cliffs

A slingshot of cheese led to her demise. How witchy and wild.
Goliath of tactical talents and impenetrable mind, and they say today
she stands upright in full armor at Cairn Knocknarea, still refuses

to lay down for anyone, even in the afterlife, tenacity and resilience
kneaded, fully risen earth and rock, formidable femme fatale, forever
facing her enemies, spear erect eternally in her gripped hand

204   Old World Wings

Lies about how your 17-year-old Brother Died (The Troubles)

It was a lie, of course, fourteen killed,
twenty-six shot on Bloody Sunday
      Wednesdays, Fridays, Tuesdays too
gore coated with 3,000 civilians

      history thornier than potato
famines, the difference, for instance,
      between being captured
and being blown to bits

      the difference between lack of
and denial of, between perished
      and this young eyeball
fused to plastered wall

      butchering kids caught
on camera, *on camera,* yet still,
      "it didn't happen that way"
mouths of those squeezing triggers spill

      the difference between peacekeepers
and regiments, the difference between
      being told your 17-year-old
brother died "attacking," protesting

      and learning the truth of a shell
torn through his upper rear thigh
      arrowed straight up his ribcage
a bullet whose only path is from behind

of someone not facing, but struggling
on hands and knees, crawling away, fingers reaching
the difference between self-defense
and teaching a lesson by slaughtering

teenagers in their own neighborhoods
near Sunday morning stoops, Stigmata potted
plants, red clover, next to pious Easter lilies
prostrating in front yards, in church grottos

Summer Solstice

We are from Wales, she declares
after they both sit down
next to my pack I share
with the cliff's chilled bench.

Forty-nine years we've been married,
his camera hangs around his neck,
I congratulate them on this feat,
they ask me where I'm from.

She smiles when I answer, and begins to sing
of muddy rowed Ohio boats, her merry mouth
joyful after glories, fine with missing sun's
slipping behind grey glimmer clouds,

climbing summit of solstice,
sea aster, clover, and cowslip
dusk watercolors painting five decades
of sharing benches with the same person

Old Men Don't Cry (Song of Arranmore)

after Jerry Early's "I'll Go"

North-northwest pounding snow
sleet-smacked downpour
bending bright red painted flowers
dotting seashore's saltwater veins
thick tongued island men
did what must be done
eight said, "I'll go," stepped forthright
for eighteen sailors stranded by storm
muscling waves cliff high, hunkering
black gales' howling ice spit, sharpened
into Donegal darts until twenty-six
were bow-brought, tales of survival
beaded for lighthouse wampum, spirits
lingering low tide, foothold fracture,
jut of joint, they said back then, *old men don't cry*
until their grandchildren's Arranmore
mouths sing briny ballads of blood born sea
marine melodies of bone mist sky

Pillage

full, glass-eyed fish

on bronze plate

      presented each night

promise of purity

assurance of abstinence

      until the eve

the slippery body

angles peculiarly

      from the most

      terrible bite

It's Like This: The Cattle Raid of Cooley

(Content Warning - the Cattle Raid (Táin) story is ancient and brutal, gory and descriptive).

1. *Afterglow*
It begins with royal entanglement in thick rugs, who has more, counting livestock, possessions with stones and pebbles, the consensus - equal, more or less… except for one fair bull

2. *Party*
Queen Maeve's anger slashed through her eyes like a stab to her side, sent her men far and wide to mead merriment, greased bird, thick salmon sealed deal, one loose tongue revealed their violent backup plan, record scratch, party over, tongues fed to dogs, heads turned into hurling balls

3. *Magic*
Poets always have red lips in these stories, and endless black eyelashes sweeping watercress eyes, Scottish soothsayers, "Poets are dangerous," said the Queen, even more than the dark arts of scratching into oak trees, Ogham marked magic, river knowledge in rushing fjords, casting drowning spells, containing all power unknown

4. *Hound*
Only 17, Scotland studied, Cuchulainn cracked skulls of bully boys, whacked and rolled them down the road, brains spilling into mile markers, he scooped the guts of the King's dog before savagely smearing the snout, when the King fell to his knees, sobbing for his soft companion, Cuchulainn felt a strange pang…offered himself as the King's new hound

5. *Macha*
There is always before, and in this before, men boasted and bragged, a piss contest of fastest horses, a drunk blurted, "my wife would take them all"; *prove it*, they demanded, "she's with child…twins" *too late*, claim laid and she was brought to

them, onlookers laughing, jeering her rounded belly and arched back, horse nostrils snorting hot musk air at her jawline, she held her protruding stomach and outran both steeds, collapsed to give birth, with legs apart, the spurned goddess Macha looked straight into the Ulstermen's eyes and cursed them as she died

6. *Beard*
One-man army, the "little puke" teenager jeered for not having a beard, he plucked sweet blackberries to smear across his chin in sticky purple goatee, then split and cleaved men in half, cut off their heads and flung them over the trees for fun, all other men useless under Macha's curse, perfect for Maeve's army to ravage, burn, and plunder while hound sharpened stones with his jagged teeth, sat naked in the snow, composed poems about his foes

7. *Morrigan*
Spiked holly javelin, another begged him, "please do not kill my brother," so he squeezed his brother's bowels instead, warrior after warrior taken out, until a young maiden adores, "oh, how I love your courage," then shapeshifts into slithering eel, growls into howling wolf, balloons to stampeding cow, yet he stomped, stoned, and split all three, grabbed his Gae Bolga like Negan's Lucille, sodomized a man whose bloodcurdling screams made miles of cattle flee and then he was quite tired, so he composed another poem, about being tired, then slipped into a daytime dream, one of a toothless one-eyed crone milking a cow, scaly hands like rooster feet

8. *Lugh*
Green cloak, black shield, five-pronged spear, his father chants over his body, swathed in herbs and healing, magic mushroom's mycelium juice rubbed into every wound, three

days later, he rose, three of course, put on his war clothes, blades on chariot wheels like a Scorpion from *Grease*, armor for horses, spikes and barbs too, sickle, gold headband, straps and wax gut to keep him in tact, his rage so great, he began to quiver and shake, insides went out, bones twisted backwards, veins became venom, face turned fire, eyes sucked in and popped out, ink blood geyser from his crown like Kali born from Durga, he sliced crowds left and right, piling corpses, bouncing heads, legs flying in fright

9. *Dandy*
he cleaned up, dressed in silk, purple, gold, parted hair with dyed roots, who could defeat him? only skin hardened Scotland studied Ferdia, who refused to fight his friend until Maeve got in his head, now in the fjord, Ferdia taunts, "fancy dandy boy…a puff of fart in the wind," three days of knives and swords slicing holes fists punch through, hacking off flesh slung on boulders, composing verses in between until a sharp bird's flitter catches Cuchulainn's eye and Ferdia's blade sunk chest deep ran river red, draped guts like slasher Spanish moss, he stumbled, curled his ham toe, hurled his Gae Bolga straight at Ferdia, and it's like this, hellraiser barbs snap out, can't be removed without rupturing body apart, so he carried Ferdia in his arms, crying, "I hate to see you Gae Bolgaed" kissing his blood brother's face, guts smeared across the clover

10. *Even*
Finally, the Ulster men wake from Macha's slumber, bathed in salmon-filled revenge rivers, salved in herb, transforming into thousands of thick necked grisly men licking their spears, Cuchulainn, now more space than form, more wounds than flesh, too jacked to join, feels forlorn FOMO as refreshed Ulsters slice, dice, slit, dissect, mangle, and tear men left and

right, three hilltops leveled flat, the King's fair blonde bull and Maeve's borrowed brown, the one this was all about, shook the earth under their snort clouds, clash of horns, fighting day and night until brown threw white's remains in the fjord; then he was done, never Maeve's for a moment, dragging himself and his loosened guts back until he reached his land, took one last breath and dropped dead. Cuchulainn watched this all unfold, began to wonder what it was all for, all this carnage and destruction, all this blood and brains, he had done his duty until Ferdia…what futility fighting over possessions, "farts in the wind," in the end, there was no bull left for either King or Queen, so at least they were finally even now, they both agreed

and they never spoke of it again

Note: Gae Bolga is a special multi-barbed spear of death; all story themes, characters, and dialogue quotes are from the Táin Bó Cúailnge

Generally Useful

I – "Price one-penny"

Quinine and iron tonic. Spirit animator.
Digestion improver. Blood purifier.
Nerve strengthener. Disease remedy.
Mental worry eraser. Chemist sold.

II - Want ads

Wanted – "a well-educated young man to be a reporter"

Wanted – "a smart, respectable girl, about 15, to clean (and make herself generally useful)"

*from *Londonderry Standard* Newspaper, Aug 1887, The Guildhall Derry

In America, this would be a Fenced Tourist Trap

2,000-year-old
Celtic cross curved
smooth ogham marked
butterknife, revered rock
slab, no fences, no gates, no
keep offs, just a small grassy
knoll behind a winding wall
of stone, no one around, no
sound except valley's wind
whistling *my holy*
perfection, that's all

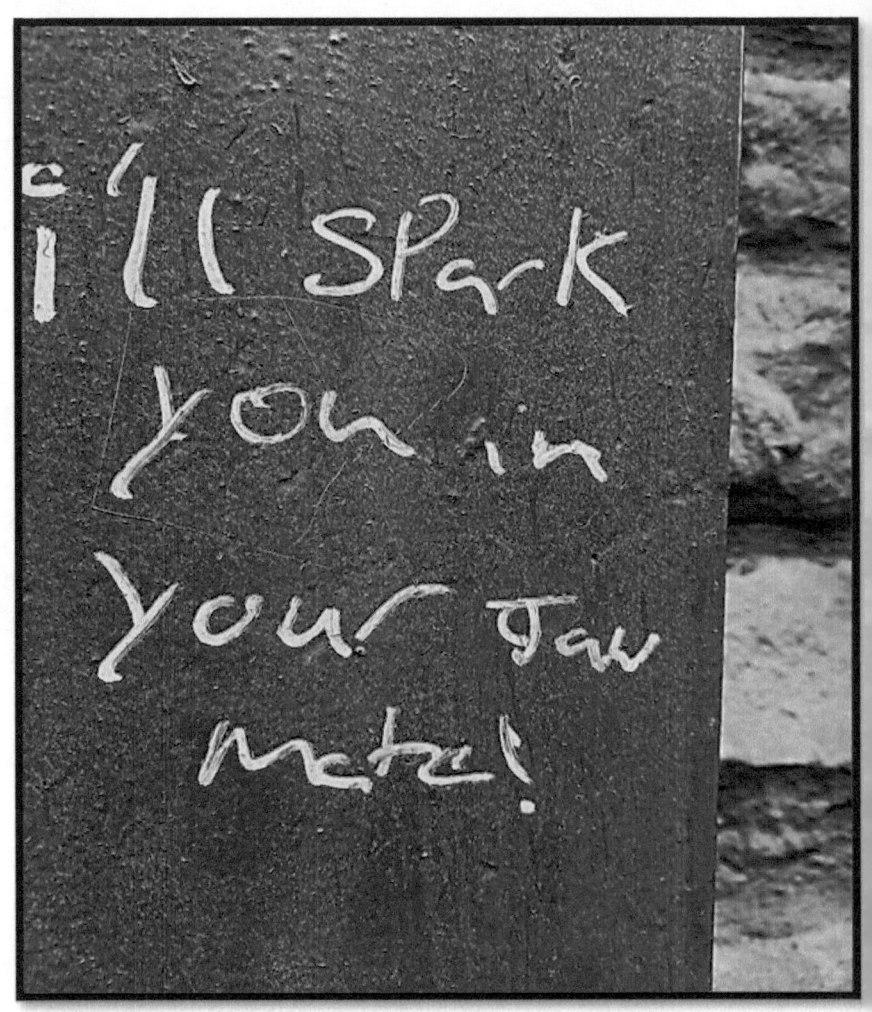

A Nietzschean Response to St. Patrick

Here is a fun take, Ireland never had snakes in the first place,
        Priest Patrick escaped
being kidnapped and enslaved, he never chased out
        any poor snakes for Pete's sake
and landlords gave "notice" in the valley by fire eviction
        lighting up thatched roofs
into burning Celtic candles and when I asked
        if they also had Mass Shootings
she shook her head, "guns are illegal, we don't have school
        shootings here like you do, we don't love guns…
that's an American thing" and on our way
        to Fish-n-Chips this wiry dude in ripped jeans,
flannel, spaghetti slim legs stretched into slack
        double Dutch jump ropes, guitar napping on lap
starts to sing in a 90s grunge voice
        except not Mudhoney or Pearl Jam
but *Do you believe in life after love* by Cher

acorn acoustic
matching blood orange stringy hair
his ginger goatee

When I Learn Enya's Castle is 20 Minutes Away

If I knocked on Enya's arched door
      I would follow her through
strange moon gardens, tourmaline talisman
      fountains pouring every corner
we would trace this maze of moments, unravel
      these cliffs with sun's gold threads

If I knocked on Enya's arched door
      wind would whisper chestnut bangs
our almond eyes earth-colored maps
      would gaze at feather paper,
China rose petals, hyssop, lavender,
      green tea from far and away

If I knocked on Enya's arched door
      I would falter, then ask to see her piano
and she would politely shake her head no
      in a most mesmeric way, speak longingly
of her bees and dancing sheep, evermore
      and then it would be time to go

If I knocked on Enya's arched door
      she would sail me out with gate's
closing clink, shore's stirring storm
      muting doves' whistles, starlings' chirps
piano keys pressed in night's candlelight wax
      sauntering my rainy way home

Heaven in a Long Room

Enter the gateway, this archway of books.
Oral histories preserved into books.
Inhale autumn leaves, ink quills, leather satchels.
Cotton cords tenderly hold fine fragile books.

Look - Ireland's oldest surviving harp!
Tomes made of willow and oak, musical books.
Follow the black wrought iron staircase spiral.
Long ladders stretch erect to volumes of books.

This room is a real working library!
This is the Sistine Chapel of books.
15th century word rapture on earth.
Dark academia exaltation of books.

Samuel Beckett and Oscar Wilde drew deep breaths.
Jonathan Swift and Bram Stoker read these books.
Right here, I mean, these guys read them *right here.*
Their fingertips traced *these* poetry books.

And maybe those over there, rough hands reached,
glided smooth, glazed banister's stretch of books.
No doubt now, bliss smells of old paper and wood.
Narrative Nirvana in 200,000 books.

Book of Kells

Iona burned, pillaged, plundered, monks
murdered by Viking villains, monastery destroyed
hand-written volumes, swollen folio tucked thick
magic spell book of curved letters laid to vellum
painstaking prayer on parchment, ochre, precious
inlaid stones, intricate treasure scrolls, yellow halos

no beard for malachite St. Mark, no evangelist halos
just bird heads, closed hands, crushed carpet monks
stone church concealed for 1200 years by precious
angels shrouded under plunder, all that's destroyed
ten times over, callous iron weapons to soft vellum
lime-soaked skin of 185 young calves, layered thick

lapis lazuli and gypsum teal, hardened sap thick
packs every page, St. John's eagle draped in halos
double wings, triskeles, chalices, vine scroll vellum
root colored, quilled and filled by teenage monks
hair roughly scraped off as all was destroyed
knots, crushed leaves, epic Zen tangles, precious

Chi Rho cats chasing rats eating, holding precious
eucharist in pointed teeth, perfect pigment thick
Gospel gripped in St. Matthew's cloak, undestroyed
inkpot sand paints, bird heads, whirligigs, no halos
focus and devotion of angel-shouldered monks
spoon bent over wooden desks, birthing in vellum

untouched by profane fingertips, willow thin vellur
in square lit case, holy altar, Latin liturgy preciou
survivor, lime-soaked skin, calf tonsure of monk
Chi Rho contrast triskele, fair yellow curls of thic
haired-Christ, flying saucer aqua eyes, copper halo
throaty Jack kept King of clubs; hearts destroye

earliest evidence of Madonna, queens destroye
goddesses burned in bark, lichen, resin for vellur
immortal peacocks, resurrecting snakes, no halo
charred clays, black iron salt, powdered preciou
stains gritty under youth's nails, stamina, eyes thic
with thorny hormones, young calves, fresh monk

who left notes, *I'm hungry, I'm cold,* preciou
blood, mass mistakes, thick fjords, swollen halo
walnut vellum, monks' alchemy never destroye

234 Old World Wings

Plans

for Dolores

fell through her hands
supplication on loose soil
defiant dirges on unguarded
precipice, kneeling, rocking
back and forth, her splintered
stricken ship a shaken lament
trickling murmur shapeshifts
into keening tongue
implores the apparitions
sea songs for the faithful
departed, a requiem
for her keen grip
to salvation, devotion
dug under her fingernails

Shamrock Wool

Rolling sheep, curly sheep, fluffy knotty yarn of sheep, church bell sheep, fence line sheep, wind, salt, and seagull sheep, Gaelic poet bard sheep, smoke a pipe fluffball sheep, sheared tale teller sheep, peaty cotton chieftain sheep, Princess Ulster, Munster sheep, dag on dag off misty sheep, Appalachian valley sheep, raddled rumen solstice sheep, boggy marsh and forest sheep, click clack cliffhanger sheep, invisible cloak sheep, yin and earth, teet and lanolin sheep, wool and horn, tongue and grass sheep

under the willows prayer sheep, old stone hut and thatched roof sheep, cloved and cloven orange sunset sheep, sheep with names like Gráinne and Catríona, Fionn mac Cumhaill sheep, shamrock flock of sheep, salmon gimmer sheep, ancestral mythical monkfish sheep, trinity spellbound sheep, shapeshifter storybook sheep, weathered and wethered leaping sheep, dancing dams and *sidhe* sheep, hay hop along mischief sheep, sheepish sheep, sheep who weep, don't care sheep, don't wear sheep, sheep who sleep, sheep who roll over and can't get back up, all four legs pointed up to clouds above, sheep who lay and wait for farmer's flip, pathetic bleating lament sheep, have you ever wondered, are we the shepherd or are we the sheep?

The Faery Bridges

Dear *sidhe*, stir in your sea aster, firelight
your woods with hypnotic lanterns, whisper
through moonlight's mycelium under leafy
ferns, bright cherries, dusk berries, dance
over the drumlins and burlap briar, hum
your wingspans like starlings, shapeshift
against clear light of sky, hobnob, bewitch
us, spin dew into shimmer, give
us stumbling humans reason not to disturb
your paths, not to uproot your nestled dwelling
places, magic mushroom us
into fearing your faery vengeance, flicker
at your sweet smidgen red doors
at base of oak trees, in lighthouse walls
overlooking mist of crashing sea, pixie dust
these violet wildflowers, cobble
undergrowth and moss, knit
tulip stories that delight and make
children behave, linger
orb realms of uncertainty, give
reason to the unexplained, weave
soft solace ribbons into cowed corridors
of grief's caverns, assure huddled husks
spoon-bent some silk thread, some wave
of magic wand what was lost is now hand
in hand with the "water and the wild"
one enchanting world where there is no weeping,
where sweet sprouts vine in mused mischief,
wander in innocence, instead of sleeping

References

- *School of Athens* - "there's nothing shameful..." and "you're blocking my light" from Diogenes: The Lives and Opinions of Eminent Philosophers by Diogenes Laertius (3rd century CE) and Archetypes of Wisdom, Douglas Soccio, 5th edition, 2018.
- Photographs on pgs. 10 and 52 taken by author at the Vatican Museum in Vatican City, March 2011.
- Photographs on pgs. 74, 75, and 243 taken by author at the Louvre in Paris, France, March 2008.
- Photographs on pg. 93, 246, and 249 taken by author at the Rodin Museum, Paris, France, March 2008.
- *Orthodox Physical* - Hebrew from B'nai Mitzvah Academy.
- Photograph of Zuzanna Urbanová taken by author in Třebíč, December 2007, permission for use granted by her son.
- *Franceska* – partially inspired by Director of the Finkler Institute of Holocaust Research, Judy Baumel-Schwartz's work, Bar-Ilan University.
- Photograph on pg. 132 taken by author; reprint of *Madonna with Green Cushion* by Andrea Solari (Solario), found in Krakow, Poland gift shop.
- *A Conversation with Queen Maeve* - "lets the soft animal of herself love what she loves" from Mary Oliver's line, "You only have to let the soft animal of your body love what it loves." Wild Geese, Dream Work, 1986.
- *Song of Arranmore* - after "I'll Go," Jerry Early, performed live at Early's Bar June 2023, https://earlys.bar/ill-go-song/599316 Records DK, 2015.
- Photograph of Girl in Gas Mask and Photograph of "You are Now Entering Free Derry" taken by author of photo displays at the Museum of Free Derry, June 2023.
- Photograph of "Spitfire Paddy" taken by author of photo display at EPIC The Irish Emigration Museum, June 2023.

- Photographs on pg. 184 and 230 taken by author at Trinity College in Dublin, Ireland, June 2023.
- *It's Like This: The Cattle Raid of Coolidge* - "Poets ar dangerous"; "fancy dandy boy…a puff of fart in the wind"; " hate to see you get Gae Bolgaed"; "little puke"; from inspire retelling from Titley, Alan, and Coveney, Eoin, *The Táin*, Litt Island Books, pgs. 30; 116; 131; 161, 2023; other referenc from Dr. Niamh Hamill's research on Táin Bó Cúailng Bundoran, Institute of Study Abroad Ireland, June 2023.
- *Generally Useful* - found poem and photo of Londonder Newspaper, Aug 1887, taken by author at The Guildhall Derr
- *The Faery Bridges* - partially inspired by Catherine Pierce excellent poem, "Entreaty," published in Danger Day Saturnalia Books, 2020; "water and the wild" from The Stol Child, William Butler Yeats, The Wanderings of Oisin a Other Poems, London: Kegan Paul & Co., 1889.

About the Author

Photo by Anne Von Koschembahr

A.M. Hayden is an award-winning Full Professor of Humanities, Philosophy, and World Religions. She served as Poet Laureate for Sinclair College from 2021-2025. Nominated twice for a Pushcart Prize and Winner of the River Heron Review Editors' Prize, she lives on a windy little farm with her family and their many rescues, including their blind, three-legged pup Vinny Valentine.

Hayden's other poetry books include American Saunter: Poems of the U.S. (FlowerSong Press, 2024) and How to Tie Tobacco (Wild Ink Publishing, 2025). Hayden loves words, nature, and having a passport that resembles a tattooed sailor. Follow her @windychickenpoet on the social things and at https://windychickenpoet.com/

Acknowledgments

First and always to God/Great Mystery, *thank you* is my prayer every day. Abigail Wild (Wild Ink Publishing) for saying: "We love your poetry." Natalie Welsh (Syncopation Literary Journal) and Dawn Terpstra (River Heron Review) for penning gorgeous and thoughtful blurbs. Dr. Niamh Hamill, living goddess, for your wisdom and knowledge cup that runneth over the cliffs and valleys of Eire, your fan-fire-tastic blurb, and taking care of us little chickens.

River Heron Review for choosing "Roma Museum" as their Poetry Prize Finalist (2023) and "The Faery Bridges" as their Editors' Prize Winner (2024). Lefty Blondie Press for selecting "Bonfire of the Vanities (Venus)" as a semi-finalist for their Broadside series (2025), Both Teresa Berkowitz (Tangled Locks) for featuring "Women have always said Sorry" (2023) and Katie Darby Mullins (The Apologist) for featuring "Plans" (2025) during National Poetry Month. A huge thank you to Samantha Terrell (Shine Poetry) for nominating "When You Said 'No' to Seeing the David" for the Pushcart Prize (2025).

Dr. Tom Martin for historical feedback, bone-dry humor in Czechy and Polska, and charming notes to the manuscript. Merci beaucoup to my knowledgeable colleague for her *jolié* French notes. Dr. Jenny Caplan, gratefully, for making sure I knew my "Shabbos" from my "Shabbat" and my "Tallis" from my "Tallit." Drs. Melissa and Ed Burkley for Italy edits and so much more.

Angela Yuriko Smith, Furaha Henry-Jones, and Jamey Coyote Dunham, my poetry cheering section from the start. Edward Vidaurre and FlowerSong Press for being the first to take chance on me, I will thank you in every book forever.

Josie Alford and her lovely poetry videos, which inspired several forms in this collection - check this adorable Brit kitten out and become her poetry pal. Karel Pančocha for making me feel at home and being the Czechy crush for everyone. Anne for showing me Paris in full *Amélie* style and for the author photo. Shelly for our fun Italy adventures and cheers to more.

Jimmy, without you, none of this would be possible. Thank you for making us a team and your all-the-way-in support for my love of writing. Our daughters, forever and always, it is all for YOU, my big-time loves, to the moon and back, a bazillion times. Finally, for the readers of this collection, *Grazie, Merci mille fois, Děkuji,* and *Go raibh maith agat.* Thank you for traveling with me and spending time with my heart.

The End

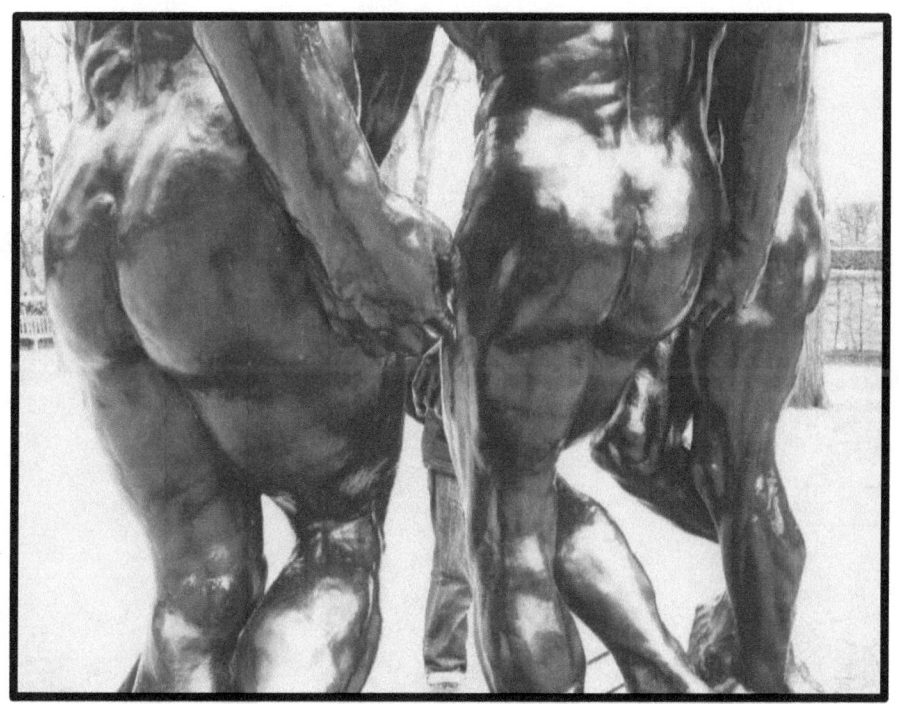

www.ingramcontent.com/pod-product-compliance
Lightning Source LLC
Chambersburg PA
CBHW021223130626
46554CB00004B/1335